Your Amazing Itty Bitty Book of Astrology

15 Key Questions People Ask About Astrology

Carol Pilkington

Published by Itty Bitty Publishing
A subsidiary of S & P Productions, Inc.

Copyright © 2015 Carol Pilkington

All rights reserved. No part of this book may be reproduced or transmitted in any form or by any means, electronic or mechanical, including photocopying, recording or by any information storage and retrieval system, without written permission of the publisher, except for inclusion of brief quotations in a review.

Printed in the United States of America

Editor: Jan Onofrio

Itty Bitty Publishing
311 Main Street, Suite E
El Segundo, CA 90245
(310) 640-8885

ISBN: 978-1-931191-55-5

I dedicate this book to Jim Sher of the Sher Institute of Astrology & Metaphysics for all that he has taught me over the years and for his friendship, support, care and guidance.

Suzy Prudden, thank you for your loving support and friendship. Thank you to all those in the Rockstar Mastermind that helped me come up with the questions in this book.

Table of Contents

Question 1	What is the Difference Between Astronomy and Astrology?
Question 2	What is the History of Astrology?
Question 3	How Do the Planets Affect or Influence Us?
Question 4	Why Should I Believe in Astrology?
Question 5	Why did the Church Prohibit Astrology?
Question 6	Why Does Astrology Get Such a Bad Rap?
Question 7	Is It a Sin to Practice/Follow Astrology?
Question 8	Will I Betray My Faith if I Follow Astrology?
Question 9	Is Astrology an Occult Practice?
Question 10	What is the Birth Chart?
Question 11	Is My Destiny, Based On Where the Planets Were When I Was Born, Written in Stone?
Question 12	If I Follow Astrology, Does That Mean I'm Not Responsible For Anything?
Question 13	What is the Difference Between Predictive Astrology and Person-Centered Astrology?
Question 14	Why Do the Horoscopes in the Newspapers Seem More Accurate Sometimes And Less Accurate at Other Times?
Question 15	What Can Astrology Do for Me?

15 Key Questions People Ask About Astrology

Question 1

What is the Difference Between Astronomy and Astrology?

For several centuries now, scientists have made many attempts to downplay and debunk astrology. However, astrology actually gave birth to physical sciences.

1. Astronomy – is the scientific study of the movement of the stars and planets.
2. Astrology – is the study of the influence those heavenly bodies and their movements have on humankind.
3. Astrology is the bridge between the outer world and the inner world.

Modern Astronomy did not exist before the 17th century. There were no real astronomers before the late 1600s, with some exceptions. Before then, astronomers were mostly called astrologers.

What is the difference between astronomy and astrology?

Prominent Astrology Visionaries and Practitioners:

- **Johannes Kepler (1571-1630)** was a key figure in the 17th century scientific revolution, having made significant contributions to astrology. He is known for many significant discoveries such as the laws of planetary motion, and was the first to derive the birth year of Christ that is now universally accepted.

- **Galileo Galilei (1564-1642)** was a practicing astrologer, who not only found himself under house arrest by the church for his views, but also experienced considerable criticism by later science writers for his astrological work.

Question 2

What is the History of Astrology?

Astrology has been around since the beginning of time when man first looked up and saw patterns in the sky.

1. Actual astrology came about during the Babylonian Period. It was used to advise the king on matters of war, famine, peace and so forth. Therefore, whatever happened to the king also happened to his subjects.
2. The Assyrians conquered the Babylonians around 1300 BC, during which a new phase of astrology developed. These ancients named the Constellations.
3. Much of astrology today is based on the relationships these constellations have with the seasons. This is known today as Tropical Astrology, and is the type of astrology mostly used in the West today (Western Astrology).
4. The Greeks were responsible for incorporating mythology into astrology. That is how the names of the planets we are familiar with today came into existence.

What is the history of astrology?

- Babylonian Astrology was the first known system of astrology and came about in the 2nd millennium BC.
- By the 1st century BC, two varieties of astrology were in existence; one that required the reading of horoscopes in order to establish precise details about the past, present and future; the other being theurgic (literally meaning 'god-work'), which emphasized the soul's ascent to the stars.
- It wasn't until the early 20th century that humanistic or psychological astrology came about. One of the most famous pioneers of this type of astrology was Dane Rudhyar. He was the most influential, by far, in moving astrology from a determinism (predictive) approach to a philosophical one. He paved the way for astrology to be used as a tool to assist us in discovering our purpose. "Astrology for the Seeker is the lamp which illuminates the darkness so that The Path may be seen."

Question 3

How Do the Planets Affect or Influence Us?

If we can understand that everything in the universe is made up of energy, then it is only reasonable that anything and everything in the universe as we know it has an effect and influence, including the planets.

1. The Sun – We get vitamin D from the Sun – Therefore, it has an effect on us physically.
2. The Moon – Has an energetic influence on the ocean tides – therefore it has an effect on Earth. Since we are 75% water, the moon also has an effect on us.
3. Both the Sun and Moon are Luminaries and yet for simplicity sake, they are categorized with the planets.

We often don't want to acknowledge how something we cannot see may influence us because that would imply that we have no control or free will. Astrology doesn't rule, it explains.

How Do the Planets Affect or Influence Us?

- It is not only because the planets have a geomagnetic influence on us that everything happens.
- The geomagnetic influence is simply one of many things to be factored into human behavior.
- The term, "as above, so below" comes from the Emerald Tablet which states, "That which is above is the same as that which is below..." For more information go to http://www.themystica.com/mystica/articles/a/below_above.html.

Question 4

Why Should I Believe in Astrology?

Please don't believe in astrology. Yes, that is what I said. For to believe in anything, including astrology, is to take another's word.

1. Investigate. I strongly recommend investigating into the nature of any subject matter to come to one's own understanding about this or any other topic.
2. Only one's own experience can be the testimony on the validity or truth of anything.

All too often we depend on others, whether it is written or spoken, to give us certainty. In doing so, we give over all authority to those outside ourselves and weaken our own ability to discern and discover.

Why Should I Believe in Astrology?

- Don't believe in anything.
- Investigate everything for yourself.

Question 5

Why Did the Church Prohibit Astrology?

During the Dark Ages, Roger Bacon, a Franciscan Friar (c.1214-1294), was one of the greatest minds of the thirteenth century. He was a proponent of astrology.

1. Bacon's view, as was the view of Thomas Aquinas, was that the Church did not denounce astrology as a whole, but did reject the fatalism and determinism of some practitioners. The fear was that astrology left no contingent for judgment or free will.
2. It is a misnomer that the Church denounced astrology. Through much of our early history the Church used astrology.
3. To read more on this go to: http://capricorn.bc.edu/siepm/DOCUMENTS/BACON/Bacon_Opus%20Majus%20I.pdf

Why Did the Church Prohibit Astrology?

- As Bacon wrote in his Opus Majus (p.150) "The characteristic of false mathematic (at the time the words mathematician and astronomer were interchangeable with astrologer) was to assert that through the powers of the constellations all things took place of necessity.
- No place was left for contingent matter, for judgment, or free will. Such a view of nature was condemned not only by theologians, but also by philosophers.
- Aristotle and Plato, Cicero and Pliny, Avicenna and Albumazar were unanimous in holding that free will remained uncoerced by the motions of heavenly bodies.
- True mathematicians and astrologers lay down no necessity, no infallibility, in their predictions of contingent events. What they do is to consider the way in which the body may be affected by celestial things, and the way in which the body may act upon the mind in private affairs or public, always without prejudice to the freedom of the will."

Question 6

Why Does Astrology Get Such a Bad Rap?

The Church, at one time, fully embraced astrology and the three Magi were highly respected astrologers and established the significance of the nativity by following a star.

1. However, during the latter part of the Renaissance, the worldviews and beliefs of the Church were challenged. The Church, therefore, took drastic measures, burning Bruno, a Dominican Friar and astrologer, at the stake, and put Galileo under house arrest.
2. As the movement of science emerged, there was a political compromise with the Church. It was agreed that science would be allowed to continue without penalty as long as it maintained its investigation in the pragmatic physical realm. The Church would have domain over the spirit, soul and morality of the Being, etc.
3. The Church and Science would respect the other's political and philosophical turf.

Why Does Astrology Get Such a Bad Rap?

- Until the middle of the Renaissance, there was little conflict between religion, astrology and science.
- Astrology was sacrificed for political reasons.
- The Catholic Church actually has the largest astrological library in the world.
- The Church began to distance itself from astrology and therefore renamed the Magi to the Three Kings.
  To read more about this fascinating story go to:
  http://www.astrologyhoroscopereadings.com/astrology-science-history.html
- Astrology, being a spiritual science dealing with both the outer and inner world, was sacrificed in order to maintain the separation of religion and science.

Question 7

Is it a Sin to Practice/Follow Astrology?

This question has been asked on and off throughout the centuries and will continue to be.

1. Many Christian astrologers have come to embrace the validity of astrology.
2. They have found astrology actually enhances and compliments their beliefs and spiritual practice.
3. Life is a magical mystery and astrology can serve as a tool and guide in conjunction with any spiritual practice.

I hope that throughout this book I have shed some light on how and why astrology has been so misunderstood.

Is it a Sin to Practice/Follow Astrology?

- Each person must follow their own conscience and make up their own mind.
- This book is not meant to convince, dishonor or assuage, but merely to present an historical understanding of astrology.

Question 8

Will I Betray My Faith If I Follow Astrology?

Some people have more questions about life and their purpose than any one spiritual practice and/or therapy can provide answers for.

1. There are no black and white answers to anything and there can be many complimentary sources that can help us understand our part in the bigger picture.
2. Everyone must follow their own heart in discovering those answers.
3. I have had many consultations with clients of different faiths and often they have discovered a deeper connection to Source, God, the Divine (whatever description feels best to you), and with their purpose.

Astrology is not a replacement of any belief system or spiritual practice. It can simply add another dimension to our inquiry and understanding of how and where we fit in this infinite universe.

Will I Betray My Faith if I Follow Astrology?

- Learning about astrology does not imply following it.
- It doesn't have to be either/or.
- Nothing is black or white.
- If you have a belief that excludes astrology, follow your faith.

Question 9

Is Astrology an Occult Practice?

For many years the word occult has carried with it a stigma of ominous dealings and dark forces. In reality the word occult simply means "hidden," or "secret." It has also come to mean "knowledge of the paranormal," and "knowledge of hidden things."

1. Clergy and royal courts once practiced astrology in secret. Therefore, it was hidden from the common populace for centuries. That which is hidden tends to arouse superstitions and misunderstandings.
2. Most occult practices are spiritually-based and stress doing "no harm" to others.
3. It wasn't until the late 19th and early 20th centuries that astrology began to openly and widely be taught and practiced by anyone that was interested.
4. The psychoanalyst, Carl Jung, used astrology a great deal in his practice; it wasn't until years later that he made that public through his book *Synchronicity*.

Is Astrology an Occult Practice?

- Jesus and his disciples met in secret in order for him to transmit his teachings in an undiluted manner and assist them in deepening their understanding and experience of Love so they could share it with the world.
- The Freemasons is also a society that meets in secret.
- The Rosicrucians are another group that has been shrouded in secrecy.

It is said that when a person is seeking with a deep commitment to learning, understanding and growing, they will find what they need.

Question 10
What is the Birth Chart?

The birth chart is a snapshot of where the planets were at the time of one's birth.

1. It is a circle signifying unity, which has 12 sections coinciding with the 12 signs of the zodiac. These sections are called houses. The houses represent areas of life an individual incarnates to learn.
2. The birth chart reveals the many possibilities, probabilities, and potentials one has to living life to its fullest.

As mentioned earlier, each of the planets and signs has a myriad of ways they can manifest. It is the person himself that brings the chart to life. As we live, learn and grow, we can potentially express the highest manifestation of these planets and signs through our own uniqueness.

♄

What is the Birth Chart?

- The birth chart is a map of possible potentials for the evolution of the person whose chart is being described.
- It is the individual that breathes life into the chart and makes it come alive.

Question 11

Is My Destiny, Based On Where the Planets Were When I Was Born, Written in Stone?

There is a term that sums this up quite well. *The map is not the territory.*

1. When you look at a globe or lay out a map, there are many routes you can take to arrive at a given destination. It is not until you actually travel along those routes that you experience them. Some may have obstacles and detours, others are easy and straightforward.
2. The birth chart is no different. Each person is going to experience life in their own way. That is why twins – with almost the same charts – express their lives in many different ways. Some things may be similar. However, each one will have incarnated to learn different lessons and their charts will be expressed accordingly.
3. The birth chart is merely a guide to assist in understanding how to navigate life with all its obstacles and opportunities.

Is My Destiny, Based On Where the Planets Were When I Was Born, Written in Stone?

- Nothing is written in stone.
- There are no guarantees about anything in life.
- The map is not the territory.
- As the individual is multidimensional, so too is the chart.

Question 12

If I Follow Astrology, Does That Mean I'm Not Responsible for Anything?

We all must take full responsibility for the actions and decisions we make. Events do not happen because of astrology. Events happen and each of us makes decisions according to our interpretation of said events.

1. Astrology is only one of many tools that can guide and assist us to learn and understand our unique potential and life's meaning.
2. No ethical astrologer will say that because certain planets are in certain signs and making certain connections an individual is going to have a hard life and always struggle. Nor will they say someone will have an easy life and can just rest on their laurels and everything will come their way.

It is hubris to think that we are not responsible for what we say or do based on circumstances or what we believe is fated.

If I Follow Astrology, Does That Mean I'm Not Responsible for Anything?

- We are always responsible for the way in which we perceive and deal with our circumstances.
- No one escapes responsibility.
- Blaming astrology removes personal responsibility from any event. Without responsibility, the person does not get the lesson and therefore, there is no growth.

Question 13

What is the Difference Between Predictive Astrology and Person-Centered Astrology?

Predictive astrology is the portent of possible future events in life and the world. It deals with what is called, "the mundane of life."

1. Astrology was mostly used in very early times to predict weather for the farmer to plant crops.
2. Because of the work of Dane Rudhyar in the early 20th century, astrology took into account the effects of the planets on the individual and made the individual the center of focus.
3. As our perceptions broaden, new vistas of understanding how we as unique beings contribute to what happens individually and collectively open to us.
4. Person-centered astrology addresses the individual's evolution and uniqueness so that we can begin to understand our contribution in the multi-layered universe. This can enable us to understand our interconnectedness and interdependence. Dane Rudhyar described this as, "wholes within wholes."

What is the Difference Between Predictive Astrology and Person-Centered Astrology?

- Predictive Astrology attempts to predict events in the future based on the positions of, and interactions between, earth and the planets, and the planets with each other.
- No one can predict the future with absolute certainty.
- Person-centered astrology helps us see not only our uniqueness, but how interconnected and interdependent we really are.

Question 14

Why Do the Horoscopes in the Newspapers Seem More Accurate Sometimes and Less Accurate at Other Times?

There are many facets to understanding astrology and there is no one-size-fits-all within the astrological systems.

1. Horoscopes in magazines and newspapers are merely the interpretations of one astrologer. They are based on trends of the day, as well as the archetypes that are represented in the Sun signs.
2. These interpretations are for the masses, not the individual, and should be taken with a grain of salt and for entertainment purposes only.
3. "Attributes" of the archetype of the sun sign (universal representation) indicates certain common traits that many in each sign display. Virgo, for instance, is "detail-oriented, perfectionist, and organized." However, not all Virgos display these exact qualities all the time. I tend to follow the axiom, "some, but not all."
4. Sun Signs are only one aspect of the affects of the 12 planets on each of us.

Why Do the Horoscopes in the Newspapers Seem More Accurate Sometimes and Less Accurate at Other Times?

- These types of horoscopes are generalizations made for the masses, not the individual.
- Since one size does not fit all, these types of horoscopes also help perpetuate the uneasy feeling about astrology.
- Astrologers bring themselves to their predictions – each according to their sign. So the generalities in newspaper horoscopes, as well as being general, will be influenced by the astrologer him or herself.

Question 15

What Can Astrology Do for Me?

First, astrology comes from the view that we are already whole and we are not broken; therefore, we do not need to be fixed.

1. Astrology can be a profound tool for self-awareness and understanding who we are and what our unique expression is for being in the world.
2. It can be a guide to assist us in our evolution of consciousness by discovering and revealing blind spots in our perceptions and behaviors.
3. Last, but not least, astrology can assist us to understand the nature and importance of cycles and where we are on the path of our lives. It provides us with insight into:
    a. how hard to push forward
    b. when to be still
    c. how we are learning what we have come here to learn
    d. how to make informed life adjustments

♄

What Can Astrology Do For Me?

- Astrology can contribute to understanding:
    - one's true nature
    - the process of one's evolution
    - the cycles of life through the cycles of the planets

You've finished. Before you go…

Tweet/share that you finished this book.

Please star rate this book on Amazon.

Reviews are solid gold to writers. Please take a few minutes to give us some itty bitty feedback on this book.

ABOUT THE AUTHOR

CAROL PILKINGTON is a spiritual mentor working with individuals who are in transition in life, people who are looking for deeper meaning, understanding and purpose. She teaches the power of deep inquiry into those questions that beg to be answered, questions that will unleash our true and authentic nature.

It is through Astrology and Contemplation (Meditation) that Carol embarked on a path to discover the purpose and meaning of her own life and what it means to be human. She says Astrology is archetypal in nature and reflects the universality of human behavior. It is both an esoteric science and an art. Astrology and Contemplation/Meditation are some of the tools that she has used and still uses in her own evolution. Carol has found them useful in assisting clients to actualize their fullest potential and purpose.

For more information on how you may work with Carol, please contact her by calling 818-975-0587 or through her website:

http://carolpilkington.com/contact/

Other Itty Bitty Books

The Amazing Itty Bitty Travel Planning Book: *15 Simple Steps to Keep Stress Out of Your Travel Plans* – Rosemary Workman

The Amazing Itty Bitty Weight Loss Book: *15 Simple Steps to Weight Loss Success* – Suzy Prudden and Joan Meijer-Hirschland

The Amazing Itty Bitty Food and Exercise Journal – Suzy Prudden and Joan Meijer-Hirschland

The Amazing Itty Bitty Cruise Journal – Itty Bitty Books

Get Your FREE gift from Carol Pilkington
"Create Your Perfect Day"
delivered directly to your phone.
Text 55678 - Code ITTY BITTY in message place.

www.ingramcontent.com/pod-product-compliance
Lightning Source LLC
Chambersburg PA
CBHW061304040426
42444CB00010B/2508